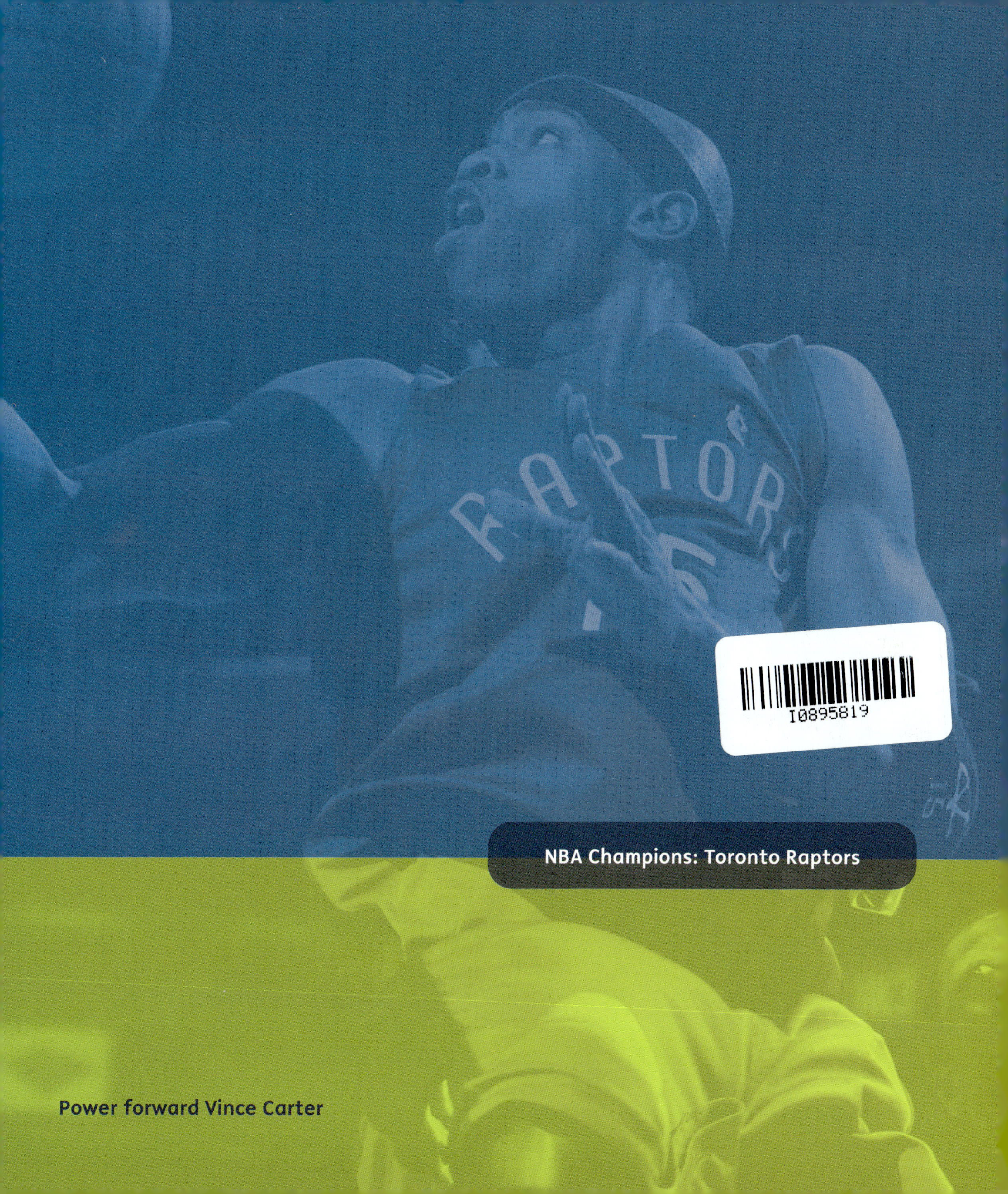

NBA Champions: Toronto Raptors

Power forward Vince Carter

Shooting guard Doug Christie

NBA CHAMPIONS

TORONTO RAPTORS

JOE TISCHLER

CREATIVE EDUCATION / CREATIVE PAPERBACKS

Center Jonas Valanciunas

Published by Creative Education and Creative Paperbacks
P.O. Box 227, Mankato, Minnesota 56002
Creative Education and Creative Paperbacks are imprints of
The Creative Company
www.thecreativecompany.us

Art Direction by Tom Morgan
Book production by Graham Morgan
Edited by Grace Cain

Images by Chris Keane/Reuters, 4; Fred Thornhill/Reuters, 16; Getty Images/ Andy Hayt, 7, 10, Barry Gossage, cover, 1, Cole Burston, 19, Fernando Medina, 15, Gary Dineen, 5, Jed Jacobsohn, 24, Mark Blinch, cover, 20; Lipofsky.com/ Steve Lipofsky, 12; Newscom/ Albert Pena/Icon SMI, 3; Rebecca Cook/Reuters, 6; Unsplash/ mwangi gatheca, 9; US PRESSWIRE, 2

Library of Congress Cataloging-in-Publication Data

Names: Tischler, Joe, author.
Title: Toronto Raptors / by Joe Tischler.
Description: Mankato, Minnesota : Creative Education and Creative Paperbacks, [2025] | Series: Creative sports: NBA champions | Includes index. | Audience: Ages 7-10 | Audience: Grades 2-3 | Summary: "Elementary-level text and dynamic sports photos highlight the NBA championship win of the Toronto Raptors, plus sensational players associated with the professional basketball team such as Scottie Barnes"— Provided by publisher.
Identifiers: LCCN 2024014034 (print) | LCCN 2024014035 (ebook) | ISBN 9798889892670 (library binding) | ISBN 9781682776339 (paperback) | ISBN 9798889893783 (ebook)
Subjects: LCSH: Toronto Raptors (Basketball team)—Juvenile literature. | Basketball players—Canada—Juvenile literature.
Classification: LCC GV885.52.T67 T57 2025 (print) | LCC GV885.52.T67 (ebook) | DDC 796.323/64—dc23/eng/20240403
LC record available at https://lccn.loc.gov/2024014034
LC ebook record available at https://lccn.loc.gov/2024014035

Printed in China

Power forward Chris Bosh

Small forward DeMar DeRozan

CONTENTS

Home of the Raptors 8

Naming the Raptors 13

Raptors History 14

Other Raptors Stars 18

About the Raptors 22

Glossary 23

Index 24

Home of the Raptors

Toronto is the largest city in Canada. It is located near Lake Ontario. The city is home to an **arena** called Scotiabank Arena. The Raptors basketball team plays there. They are the only National Basketball Association (NBA) team to play its home games outside the United States.

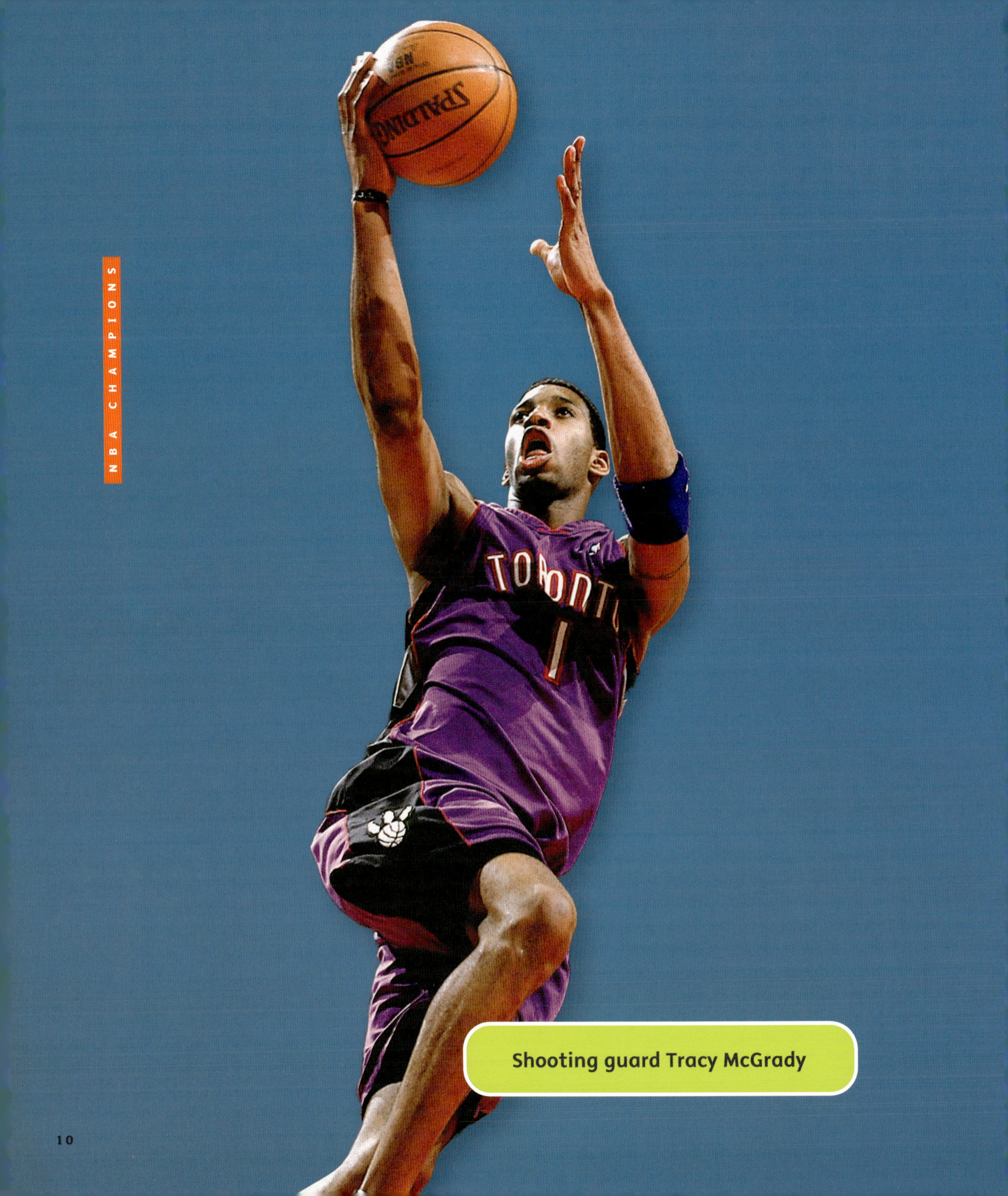

Shooting guard Tracy McGrady

The Toronto Raptors compete in the Atlantic Division. That's part of the Eastern Conference. Their **rivals** are the Brooklyn Nets and New York Knicks. All NBA teams want to win the NBA Finals and become champions.

Small forward Willie Anderson

Naming the Raptors

Toronto was awarded an NBA team in 1993. A contest was held to name the team. Raptors was chosen from a list of finalists. Influence for the name came from the popularity of the 1993 movie *Jurassic Park*. The team's first uniforms featured a big dinosaur on the front of the jersey.

Raptors History

The Raptors began play in 1995. Point guard Damon Stoudamire was the team's first draft choice. It was a good pick. He was named NBA Rookie of the Year. But the team failed to make the playoffs in its first four seasons.

High-flying forward Vince Carter came in 1998. He was well-known for his spectacular **slam dunks**. He could also score a lot of points. He was also named NBA Rookie of the Year.

Power forward Vince Carter

Point guard Kyle Lowry

He played in five All-Star Games as a Raptor. He led Toronto to its first three playoff appearances.

Toronto had many losing seasons. Point guard Kyle Lowry helped them win more games. He came in 2012. He played in six All-Star Games. Toronto made the conference finals in 2016. They lost to the Cleveland Cavaliers.

The Raptors made a big trade before the 2018–19 season. They acquired forward Kawhi Leonard. He previously won a **title** with the San Antonio Spurs. In 2019, Leonard led Toronto to their first NBA Finals appearance. They beat the Golden State Warriors in six games. The Raptors were champions for the first time!

NBA CHAMPIONS

Other Raptors Stars

The Raptors have had many other great stars. Center Chris Bosh was an **all-star** player for five seasons as a Raptor. He was a great scorer and **rebounder**. Small forward DeMar DeRozan played nine great seasons with the Raptors.

Power forward Pascal Siakam was a key player on the 2019 title team. He was named NBA Most Improved Player that year.

Power forward Pascal Siakam

Shooting guard Scottie Barnes

Point guard Fred VanVleet was a great passer. He had a lot of **assists.**

Scottie Barnes made the All-Star Game in 2024. R. J. Barrett can score points. Raptors fans hope they can help bring another championship to Toronto soon!

About the Raptors

First season: 1995–96

Conference/division: Eastern Conference, Atlantic Division

Team colors: red, black, purple, gold, and white

Home arena: Scotiabank Arena

NBA CHAMPIONSHIPS:

2019, 4 games to 2 over Golden State Warriors

TEAM WEBSITE:

https://www.nba.com/raptors/

Glossary

all-star—a player picked to play in the All-Star Game, featuring the season's top stars

arena—a large building with seats for spectators, where sports games and entertainment events are held

assist—a basketball pass that leads to a basket

rebounder—a player who catches and controls the ball after a missed shot

rival—a team that plays extra hard against another team

slam dunk—a basketball shot that is shoved through the hoop

title—another word for championship

Small forward DeMar DeRozan

Index

Anderson, Willie, 12

Barnes, Scottie, 20, 21

Bosh, Chris, 5, 18

Carter, Vince, 1, 14, 15, 17

Christie, Doug, 2

DeRozan, DeMar, 6, 18, 24

Leonard, Kawhi, 17

Lowry, Kyle, 16, 17

McGrady, Tracy, 10

Scotiabank Arena, 8, 22

Siakam, Pascal, 18, 19

Stoudamire, Damon, 14

team name, 13

VanVleet, Fred, 21

Valanciunas, Jonas, 4